Making
a Road

Focus: Systems

PETER SLOAN &
SHERYL SLOAN

A power shovel
digs the dirt.

A truck
carries the dirt.

A bulldozer
pushes the dirt.

A grader
scrapes the dirt.

A tanker
waters the dirt.

A roller
rolls the dirt.

A tar truck
sprays tar
on the dirt.